P9-EKW-985

PREHISTORIC SKIES

by Dougal Dixon

NEW
FOREST
PRESS

CONTENTS

Introduction..4

The pioneers...6

Early flying reptiles..............................8

The discovery of the pterosaurs..........10

Solnhofen—pterosaur paradise...........12

The earliest pterosaur.........................14

Big heads...16

Soft coverings......................................18

The most famous..................................20

Heads & crests.....................................22

The biggest...24

The first bird..26

Chinese "Gang of Three".....................28

Toward modern birds...........................30

Abandoning flight................................32

Since the dinosaurs.............................34

Did you know?......................................36

Summary timeline................................38

Where did they live?............................40

New discoveries...................................42

Movies, websites, & further reading...44

Glossary..46

Index...47

Acknowledgments................................48

Publisher: Tim Cook
Editor: Guy Croton
Designer: Carol Davis
Production Controller: Ed Green
Production Manager: Suzy Kelly

ISBN: 978-1-84898-331-1
Library of Congress Control Number: 2010925205
Tracking number: nfp0006

North American edition copyright
© TickTock Entertainment Ltd. 2010
First published in North America in 2010 by
New Forest Press, PO Box 784, Mankato, MN 56002
www.newforestpress.com

Printed in the USA
9 8 7 6 5 4 3 2 1

Every effort has been made to trace the copyright
holders, and we apologize in advance for any
omissions. We would be pleased to insert the
appropriate acknowledgments in any subsequent
edition of this publication.

The author has asserted his right to be identified
as the author of this book in accordance with the
Copyright, Design, and Patents Act, 1988.

PREHISTORIC SKIES

INTRODUCTION

Ever since life left the oceans back in Silurian and Devonian times, there have been things living in the air. The first land plants would have been pollinated by spores, tiny cells light enough to be carried on the winds from plant to plant. The first animals on land would have been the insects and other small arthropods, and these quickly evolved the ability to fly.

Flight is a process that involves a lot of energy. Evolution usually takes the route of least energy, and so there must have been something very advantageous about a flying lifestyle or it would never have developed.

Perhaps, like the plant spores, animals needed to travel long distances to find mates, or to find food? Flying tends to be a very fast mode of travel. Or perhaps flight developed to allow an animal to escape predators on the ground? Nowadays, when we look at the animal life of islands, we often see birds that have abandoned flight and taken up a ground-dwelling existence. Is this because there are no ground-dwelling predators on these islands, so no need to escape into the sky? This suggests that escape was an important reason for the evolution of the ability in the first place.

For whatever reason, by Carboniferous times the air was buzzing with insects of all sorts. The different concentration of gases in the atmosphere at the time meant that some of these insects were very large—imagine dragonflies the size of hawks, and roaches as big as blue jays. Flight was such a success that even today most insects have this ability.

The first vertebrates to take to the skies were the reptiles. They did not fly, but rather glided passively on the air currents. They used wings that were formed of flaps of skin supported by bony

4

struts, and were able to glide from tree to tree, or from rock ledge to rock ledge. Again, we still have this today, in the form of the gliding lizards and the flying snakes of south-east Asia.

True flight only arrived with the pterosaurs. Distant relatives of the dinosaurs, these had the power of flapping flight, using muscular wings as do the birds and the bats of today. Many types of pterosaur shared the world with the dinosaurs from the end of the Triassic period until both groups were wiped out at the end of the Cretaceous. Powered flight such as this needs a great deal of energy, and so a great deal of food. The pterosaurs had a warm-blooded metabolism, like birds and mammals, and were covered in hair to provide the insulation needed for this to work. The pterosaurs ranged from the size of sparrows to the size of small airplanes.

This lifestyle—the warm-blooded, insulated, flapping-wing flight lifestyle —was such a good idea that it evolved again, quite independently. An offshoot from the meat-eating dinosaur line developed feathered wings and an insulated body and evolved into the birds. These appeared about half way through the age of dinosaurs and shared the skies with the pterosaurs until the latter became extinct at the end of the Cretaceous period.

But the birds were luckier than the pterosaurs. Although 75 percent of bird families were wiped out along with the pterosaurs, enough survived to expand and dominate the skies as they do today.

And they are not alone. After the extinction of the pterosaurs certain mammals took to the air as well. These were not just the gliding mammals that we see in the flying squirrels and the like, but mammals that were able to fly using proper muscular wings. These were the bats. They did not compete directly with the birds, but hunted food that the birds left alone, and flew at times when the birds were resting.

There is no doubt that a flying lifestyle is very advantageous to some animals. And there will be flying animals for as long as there is life on this earth.

THE PIONEERS

While the dinosaurs, fish, and mammals were colonizing the land and the sea in prehistoric times, the sky above was buzzing with activity. Early flyers were simple organisms, but nature gradually came up with more complex designs. First came the insects, which continue to flourish today. Next came the flying reptiles, gliding creatures that evolved from ground-living, lizardlike animals. These reptiles were replaced in importance by the pterosaurs, probably the most famous of the ancient flying reptiles. Finally, the first birds appeared halfway through the time of the dinosaurs and have continued to rule the skies to this day.

AMBER PERFECTION

The best fossils come from amber preservation. When an unwary insect gets stuck in the sticky resin that oozes from tree trunks, the resin engulfs the insect and preserves it perfectly. When the tree dies and becomes buried over a long period of time, the resin solidifies and becomes the mineral we call amber. The 1994 film *Jurassic Park* was based on the premise that foreign DNA could be taken from biting insects preserved in amber to recreate the creature that was bitten. While this might not be possible today, it is an exciting concept.

THE FIRST KINGS

Meganeura was like a dragonfly but much larger—the size of a parrot. Its wings were typical insect wings, consisting of a thin sheet of chitin supported by a network of rigid veins. *Meganeura* lived in the Carboniferous Period, not long after insects first evolved.

WING AND A PRAYER

The earliest flying reptile known was the Late Permian *Coelurosauravus*. It looked very much like a lizard, but its ribs were extended to the side and supported gliding wings made of skin. The modern flying lizard of Malaysia glides in exactly the same manner as *Coelurosauravus*.

KING OF THE SKIES

By Late Triassic times, gliders like *Coelurosauravus* had been replaced in importance by the pterosaurs. These famous flying reptiles were the first vertebrates to adapt to a life of active flight. They appeared at about the same time as the first dinosaurs and became extinct at the end of the Cretaceous Period. Pterosaur wings were made of reinforced skin stretched out on an arm and an elongated fourth finger.

EARLY BIRDS

Birds such as this *Sinornis* appeared about halfway through the time of the dinosaurs, evolving from the dinosaurs themselves. Birds continue to thrive and are the main flying vertebrates today. Their wings are made of a bony structure consisting of some of the fingers fused together and supporting feathers that fan from the arms.

CARBONIFEROUS/PERMIAN	TRIASSIC	EARLY/MID JURASSIC	LATE JURASSIC	EARLY/LATE CRETACEOUS
354-290/290-248 MYA	248-206 MYA	206-159 MYA	159-144 MYA	144-65 MYA

EARLY FLYING REPTILES

The simplest kind of flight is a gliding flight—one that needs little muscular effort. All that is required is a lightness of body and some kind of structure that catches the air and allows the body to be carried along upon it, like a paper airplane. In modern times, we see this structure in flying squirrels, flying lizards, and even flying frogs. A number of flying reptiles populated the skies in Permian and Triassic times, and each one evolved independently from different reptile ancestors.

A FAMOUS FIND

A schoolboy in New Jersey discovered a famous specimen of Late Triassic *Icarosaurus*. The partial skeleton shows it to have been a lizardlike animal with long projections from its ribs. The angles at which the rib extensions lay suggested that the wings could have been folded back out of the way when the animal was at rest. The only specimen of *Icarosaurus* is now in the American Museum of Natural History in New York, having been in the private collection of its finder for many years.

SHAROVIPTERYX IN FLIGHT

When alive, *Sharovipteryx* must have been able to glide using the wings on its hind legs. This would not have been a very stable type of flight, but it was probably efficient to transport the reptile from one tree to another. Small skin flaps on the forelimbs would have helped control the flight. With the wing membrane stretched on elongated limbs, *Sharovipteryx* must have resembled a back-to-front pterosaur. Some scientists have even suggested that it may have been among the pterosaurs' early relatives.

LONG LEGS

Late Triassic *Sharovipteryx* from central Asia was a small lizardlike animal about the size of a sparrow. It had the most ridiculous-looking hind legs, each one longer than the complete length of the body. These long legs only made sense when scientists noticed the imprint of a membrane of skin stretched between the legs and the middle of the tail.

SOLAR POWERED

Kuehneosaurus, a gliding reptile that existed in western England in the Late Triassic, was very similar in structure to *Icarosaurus*. There were about a dozen wing supports (about half the number of the earlier *Coelurosauravus*), suggesting that the wings were longer and narrower and probably more maneuverable. The skin of the wings was probably rich in blood vessels, and the wings may have helped warm up the animal in the sun like a solar panel.

LONGISQUAMA

This fossil of the flying reptile *Longisquama* comes from Late Triassic central Asia. It had a completely different type of flying mechanism. A double row of long scales stuck up along the backbone, each scale forming a shallow V-shape along its midline. When spread, the scales would have overlapped like the feathers of birds (which appeared 60 million years later) to give a continuous gliding surface.

SCALES

PERMIAN	TRIASSIC	EARLY/MID JURASSIC	LATE JURASSIC	EARLY/LATE CRETACEOUS
290-248 MYA	248-206 MYA	206-159 MYA	159-144 MYA	144-65 MYA

THE DISCOVERY OF THE PTEROSAURS

T he first pterosaur fossil to have been scientifically studied was an almost perfect skeleton from the lithographic limestone quarries of Solnhofen, Germany, discovered between 1767 and 1784 (see pages 12–13). Although the skeleton was nearly complete, it was impossible to compare it with any animal alive at the time, so the find remained a mystery. Seventeen years later, the French pioneer naturalist Baron Georges Cuvier guessed that it was a flying reptile. Since that date, scientists have come up with many different ideas of what pterosaurs were and how they lived.

JURASSIC BATS?

English geologist Sir Henry De la Beche produced a drawing in 1830 showing animal life in the Jurassic (then called Liassic) sea of southern England. Life in the sea consisted of swimming reptiles, fish, and ammonites. In the air were flying pterosaurs, which De la Beche depicted as batlike creatures, with their wing membranes stretching all the way to their feet.

DEVILISH PTEROSAUR

In 1840, British geologist Thomas Hawkins published a book on the fossil sea reptiles (the ichthyosaurs and plesiosaurs) that had been discovered up to that time. The frontispiece of the book was an engraving by John Martin, an English painter of biblical and historical subjects. It was a nightmare scene in which he depicted monstrous ichthyosaurs, plesiosaurs, and pterosaurs that resembled bat-winged demons.

FURRY PTEROSAURS

A surprisingly modern interpretation of pterosaurs was drawn in 1843 by Edward Newman. He regarded them as flying marsupials. Although the mouse ears are inaccurate, the furry bodies and the predatory lifestyle are very much in keeping with how we now regard these creatures.

VICTORIAN TERRORS

The concrete pterosaurs (or "pterodactyles" as they were then called) erected on the grounds of the Crystal Palace in south London in 1854 tell us that most Victorians still viewed these creatures as winged dragons. These statues were more delicate than the surrounding statues of dinosaurs and sea animals, and despite being under constant repair they are not always on display.

SWIMMING PTEROSAURS

In 1784, some scientists put forward the idea that pterosaurs were not flying animals but swimming animals. This theory influenced many scientists and artists, including Johann Wagler, whose 1830 sketch (right) suggested that pterosaurs were an intermediate stage between mammals and birds.

SOLNHOFEN— PTEROSAUR PARADISE

Solnhofen in southern Germany has produced a treasure trove of finds—fossils in such wonderful condition that every detail of even the most delicate of organisms can still be seen. The rock is made of very fine particles and was formed under conditions totally lacking in oxygen, so no further decay took place. The technical name that geologists give to such fossil occurrences is *lagerstatten*. Only about a dozen such sites are known, and most people regard Solnhofen as the best in the world.

ANATOMY OF A LAGOON

Along the edge of the continental shelf to the north of the Tethys Ocean, a vast reef of sponges grew in deeper waters. Remains of this reef can now be found stretching from Spain to Romania. As it approached the surface, this reef stopped growing as the sponges died and coral reefs started to grow on top of them. Eventually, a series of lagoons was formed between the reef and the land. Low islands lay across the lagoon, and these were arid, with only a few scraggly plants. The stagnant water in the lagoon became poisonous and killed any animal that swam or fell into it. Because fine sediment was accumulating below, these animals were preserved almost perfectly at the bottom of the lagoon.

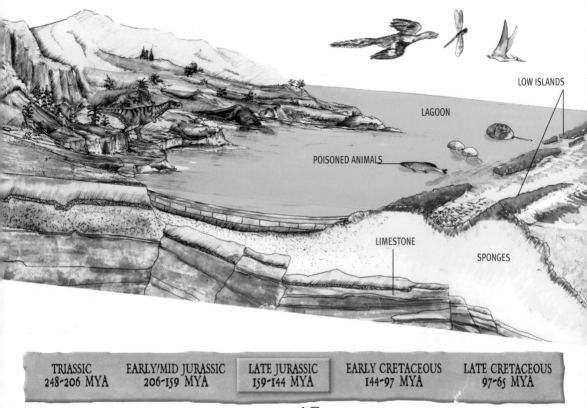

LOW ISLANDS

LAGOON

POISONED ANIMALS

LIMESTONE

SPONGES

TRIASSIC 248-206 MYA	EARLY/MID JURASSIC 206-159 MYA	LATE JURASSIC 159-144 MYA	EARLY CRETACEOUS 144-97 MYA	LATE CRETACEOUS 97-65 MYA

THE HEADLESS ONES

Many of the pterosaur fossils found at Solnhofen are without their heads.

The probable reason is that when the pterosaurs died they fell into the shallow waters along the northern edge of the Tethys Ocean.

When the pterosaurs landed on the lagoon, they floated at the surface for a while because their bodies were so lightweight.

While lying on the surface, their floating bodies began to decay and their heads, being the heaviest part, fell off first.

Eventually, after their heads had fallen off, the rest of the pterosaurs' bodies sank to the lagoon floor, where they were quickly covered by fine sediment.

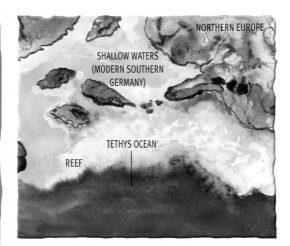

NORTHERN EUROPE

SHALLOW WATERS (MODERN SOUTHERN GERMANY)

TETHYS OCEAN

REEF

SOLNHOFEN

Over millions of years, the surface of Earth has changed due to the action of plate tectonics, the name given to the activity that occurs beneath Earth's surface. Hot magma rises, forcing our planet to tear on the surface and separating previously joined landmasses. In late Jurassic times, the area of southern Germany, including Solnhofen, lay in the shallows along the northern edge of the Tethys Ocean. This ocean separated Europe from Africa. Today all that is left of the Tethys is the Mediterranean Sea and the drying puddles of the Black Sea, the Caspian Sea, and the Aral Sea, all flanked by the mountains that were pushed out of the ground as the continents collided.

THE MODERN QUARRIES

Centuries ago, Romans excavated the fine limestone from the Solnhofen quarries to make tiles and paving stones. In the 18th century, the fine-grained surface of the rock was found to be ideal for printing. This discovery led to the rapid expansion of the quarries. Despite the fact that these quarries are famous for their fossils (not only of pterosaurs, but of early birds, small dinosaurs, lizards, and a whole host of marine animals), it takes the removal of a vast volume of rock to find one worthwhile skeleton.

CORAL REEFS

THE EARLIEST PTEROSAUR

The pterosaurs were the most important of the flying animals in Triassic, Jurassic, and Cretaceous times. Once they evolved, they quickly adopted all the features that were to remain with the group for the rest of their existence. Pterosaurs fall into two groups. The more primitive group— the rhamphorhynchoids—had long tails, short wrist bones, and narrow wings. Appearing in Triassic times, they were the first to evolve. The other group—the pterodactyloids— evolved later, toward the end of the Jurassic.

EUDIMORPHODON

Eudimorphodon had all the physical attributes of the rhamphorhynchoids. It had long, narrow wings made of skin supported by rods of gristle and a wing span of about 3 feet (1 meter). Because of its variety of teeth, it could easily catch and eat fish, and its furry body kept this creature warm and helped make possible its constantly active lifestyle.

SHORT WRIST BONES

TEETH OF DIFFERENT SIZES

FURRY BODY

AN EDUCATED GUESS

Two good fossils of *Eudimorphodon* are known. They both have the wings folded to the body, but the wing membrane has not been preserved. Nor is there any direct evidence of a furry pelt. We can, however, guess what the membrane and the fur were like by comparing the fossils with pterosaurs that were better preserved (see pages 16–17).

TRIASSIC 248-206 MYA	EARLY/MID JURASSIC 206-159 MYA	LATE JURASSIC 159-144 MYA	EARLY CRETACEOUS 144-97 MYA	LATE CRETACEOUS 97-65 MYA

THE FANTASY

Many works of fiction, including the film *One Million Years BC*, show pterosaurs carrying away heavy prey like human beings in their feet or their jaws. Even if human beings had been around at that time, the pterosaurs would have been unable to do this without severely disrupting their center of balance.

NARROW WINGS PRODUCING ACTIVE, FLAPPING FLIGHT

CATCHING PREY

Many pterosaurs caught fish, and, judging by its teeth, *Eudimorphodon* was one of them. The balance of the animal in flight was so delicate that it would not have been able to fly with a fish in its mouth. The pterosaur had to have swallowed the fish immediately to get it to its center of balance.

WING MUSCLES

Pterosaurs must have had a flying action like that of modern bats or birds (right). The arrangement of their shoulder bones and wing bones show that the muscles facilitated active, flapping flight.

LONG TAIL

BIG HEADS

Rhamphorhynchoid pterosaurs ruled the skies during the early Jurassic Period. The earliest Jurassic pterosaur known was discovered in 1828 by the famous professional collector Mary Anning. It was given the name *Dimorphodon* because of its two types of teeth. Scientists today are still in disagreement over many of its features. These disagreements are typical of our lack of knowledge of the pterosaurs in general.

BRILLIANT BEAK

Dimorphodon had two different types of teeth that were good for grabbing and holding slippery prey such as fish. The skull was very high and narrow and consisted of windows separated by fine struts of bone. The sides of the head were very likely brightly colored for signaling, just like the beaks of modern tall-beaked birds, such as puffins or toucans.

DIMORPHODON SKELETON

The skeletons of *Dimorphodon* fall to pieces and are crushed easily, because they are made up of the finest struts of bone. Nevertheless, two good Dimorphodon specimens have been found, both of them now in the Natural History Museum in London.

ON THE GROUND

We know that pterosaurs like *Dimorphodon* were very adept at flight, but we are not sure how they moved around when they were not flying. The old theory was that pterosaurs crawled like lizards, while some scientists saw them as running on their hind legs like birds, with their wings folded out of the way. However, footprints in lake sediments from South America attributed to pterosaurs show the marks of the hind feet walking in a narrow track, with marks seemingly made by the claws of the forelimbs in a wider track on each side. This suggests that pterosaurs were walking upright, using the arms like crutches or walking sticks. A final theory suggests that because of their similarity to bats, perhaps they did not come to the ground at all but hung upside down from trees.

TRIASSIC 248-206 MYA	EARLY/MID JURASSIC 206-159 MYA	LATE JURASSIC 159-144 MYA	EARLY CRETACEOUS 144-97 MYA	LATE CRETACEOUS 97-65 MYA

JURASSIC SKIES

Above the Early Jurassic shorelines the air was thick with wheeling pterosaurs. They were all of the long-tailed rhamphorhynchoid type. Within a few million years these creatures would be replaced by a new pterosaur group—the short-tailed, long-necked, long-wristed pterodactyloids.

SOFT COVERINGS
WING STRUCTURE

Most fossils are of sea-living animals, because these creatures have a better chance of falling to the seabed and eventually becoming entombed in sedimentary rocks. However, many pterosaurs lived in coastal areas or around lakes and fell into the water when they died. Sometimes, they were fossilized in environments that preserved the finest of details, such as wing membranes and furry coverings.

A MODERN INTERPRETATION?

It is often thought that birds are the modern equivalents of pterosaurs. However, the modern bat has more in common with a pterosaur than any bird—especially its membranous wings and furry covering. Pterosaurs and birds shared the Cretaceous skies, but bats did not evolve until pterosaurs died out. This in itself seems to suggest that bats rather than birds occupy the pterosaurs' niche in modern times.

WELL PRESERVED

This *Rhamphorhynchus* from the Solnhofen deposits in Germany is one of the best-preserved pterosaur fossils we have. Even the structure of its wing membrane is visible.

TRIASSIC	EARLY/MID JURASSIC	LATE JURASSIC	EARLY CRETACEOUS	LATE CRETACEOUS
248-206 MYA	206-159 MYA	159-144 MYA	144-97 MYA	97-65 MYA

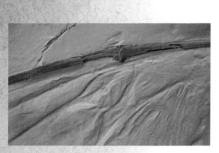

WING STRUCTURE

The wing membrane of a pterosaur was stiffened by fine rods of gristle that fanned out from the arm and hand to the wing's trailing edge. The pattern of gristle stiffening is the same as the arrangement of the flight feathers of a bird and the supporting fingers of a bat's wing.

FURRY PTEROSAUR

The fossil of the rhamphorhynchoid *Sordes*, discovered among late Jurassic lake deposits in Kazakhstan in 1971, proved what many palaeontologists had thought for a long time—that the pterosaurs were covered in hair. The sediment was so fine and the fossilization so complete that not only was the wing membrane preserved, but fibrous patches were visible on the whole of the body, except for the tail. The diamond-shaped flap of skin at the end of the long stiff tail was probably used for steering or for balancing during flight.

HOW WERE THE WINGS ATTACHED?

There is a great deal of uncertainty about just how a pterosaur's wings were attached to the animal. Some scientists think that the wings stretched from the arms and fourth finger to the body and did not touch the hind limbs. Perhaps the wings were attached to the hind limbs at the knees. Alternatively, it is possible that the wings stretched down to the ankles.

ATTACHED TO THE BODY   ATTACHED TO THE LEGS   ATTACHED TO THE ANKLES

THE MOST FAMOUS

It is *Pterodactylus* that gives the pterodactyloid group its name. In fact, pterosaurs are commonly referred to as "pterodactyls." The pterodactyloids dominated in Late Jurassic times, but there have been several different types found dating from this time, so their evolution must have been underway somewhat earlier.

PTERODACTYLUS IN FLIGHT

Most agree that pterodactyloids originally evolved from rhamphorhynchoids, but *Pterodactylus* does display several differences from the group. Its head and neck are longer than in the rhamphorhynchoids. The head meets the neck at a right angle, rather than in a straight line, and its skull is more lightly built. It has a short tail, with no steering or flying function, and its long wrist bones mean that the three fingers of the "hand" are farther down the wing.

PTERODACTYLUS FOSSIL

As with *Rhamphorhynchus*, the best specimens of *Pterodactylus* have been found in the limestone deposits of Solnhofen. They clearly show the details of the skeleton and occasionally the imprints of the wing membranes. Sometimes there is even the imprint of a throat pouch similar to that of a pelican. Other remains of *Pterodactylus* have been found in similarly aged rocks on the south coast of England and in the dinosaur-rich deposits of Tanzania in Africa.

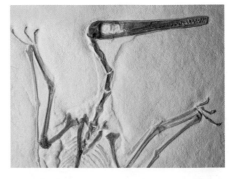

TRIASSIC 248-206 MYA	EARLY/MID JURASSIC 206-159 MYA	LATE JURASSIC 159-144 MYA	EARLY CRETACEOUS 144-97 MYA	LATE CRETACEOUS 97-65 MYA

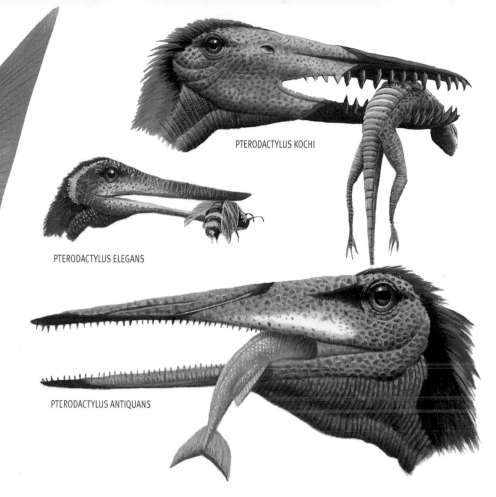

PTERODACTYLUS KOCHI

PTERODACTYLUS ELEGANS

PTERODACTYLUS ANTIQUANS

DIFFERENT HEADS, DIFFERENT FOODS

Several different species of *Pterodactylus* ruled the skies, each one adapted to a particular lifestyle and to eating a particular food. The smaller species with tiny teeth were probably insect eaters, while the bigger forms were most likely fish eaters. Six species are currently acknowledged, all discovered in Solnhofen. We used to think that there were far more, but many of these finds have subsequently turned out to be juveniles of known species.

THEORY OF EVOLUTION

When the British scientist Charles Darwin visited the Galapagos islands in the 19th century, he was struck by the variety of different beak shapes among one species of finch. Different shapes supported different lifestyles —heavy beaks for cracking seeds and short beaks for pecking insects, and so on. This revelation triggered Darwin's theory of evolution—the idea that, over millions of years, creatures could evolve to adapt to their surroundings. The variation in shape of the various *Pterodactylus* species fits in perfectly with Darwin's theory.

HEADS & CRESTS

Birds are in great abundance today. They range from perching birds and swimming birds to wading birds and hunting birds. Modern birds have a variety of different heads and beaks—deep, strong beaks for cracking nuts; long, pointed beaks for probing mud; short, sharp beaks for pecking insects; and hooked beaks for tearing flesh. This variety was just as pronounced among the pterodactyloids. During their time on Earth, they diversified into different types, with different head shapes to suit different lifestyles.

DSUNGARIPTERUS RESTORED

We can usually tell how an animal lived and what it ate by looking at its jaws. *Dsungaripterus*, which we think lived in Late Jurassic and Early Cretaceous Africa, probably ate shellfish. The narrow, pointed jaws could have been used for digging out shellfish from rocky crannies, and the shells would have been crushed by the toothlike knobs in the back of their jaws. The crest could have been brightly colored and was probably used for signaling other pterosaurs.

HIDEOUS FIND

One of the most grotesque of the pterosaurs was *Dsungaripterus*. It had a beak like a pair of upturned forceps, a battery of crushing, toothlike, bony knobs at the back of the jaws and a crest that stretched from the back of the head to the snout. It was a large pterosaur with a wingspan of more than 10 feet (3 m). *Dsungaripterus* was the first pterosaur discovered in China.

A QUESTION OF CRESTS

Many pterosaurs had spectacular crests that allowed them to signal to one another and identify members of their own species.

Tapejara was characterized by a tall, bony crest at the front of its skull, probably supporting a flap of skin behind.

TAPEJARA

Pteranodon, with its backward-pointing crest, is the most famous of the crested pterosaurs. Its crest may have helped it steer as it flew.

PTERANODON

TUPUXUARA

Tupuxuara had a crest that consisted of a vast plate of bone reaching up and beyond the back of the skull. It was full of blood vessels and so must have been covered by skin. Perhaps it had a heat-regulating function as well as being used for display.

Tropeognathus had semicircular crests on its upper and lower jaws. This crest arrangement may have helped divide the water as the pterosaur dipped into the waves for fish.

TROPEOGNATHUS

TRIASSIC 248-206 MYA	EARLY/MID JURASSIC 206-159 MYA	LATE JURASSIC 159-144 MYA	EARLY CRETACEOUS 144-97 MYA	LATE CRETACEOUS 97-65 MYA

THE BIGGEST

Pteranodon was discovered in the 1870s in the Upper Cretaceous beds of Kansas. It had a wingspan of more than 30 feet (9 m). This discovery occurred before the age of powered aviation, and science was astounded by the idea that anything this large could fly. Today its size seems fairly modest when we compare it with more recent discoveries.

THE BIGGEST —FOR THE MOMENT

The current record holder is *Arambourgiania*, a pterodactyloid that may have had a wingspan of about 39 feet (12 m). It had an extremely long neck, and when the neck bones were first found they were thought to have been the long finger bones that supported the wing. The original name given to this creature was *Titanopteryx*, but scientists had already given that name to something else, so its title had to be changed.

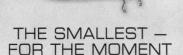

THE SMALLEST — FOR THE MOMENT

At the other end of the scale, tiny *Anurognathus* holds the record for the smallest known pterosaur. It had a wingspan of about 2 feet (60 centimeters). Its short head contained little peg-like teeth that were ideal for catching and crushing insects. Despite its short pterodactyloid-like tail, it is actually a member of the more primitive rhamphorhynchoids. Only one skeleton has been found, in the Late Jurassic Solnhofen deposits (see pages 12–13).

PTERANODON SKELETON

This partial skeleton of the giant pterosaur *Pteranodon* was found in Cretaceous rocks in Kansas. It shows a skull fragment, the bones of the wing finger, and the complete hind legs. The whole skeleton was extremely light in weight, and the bones had openings to allow oxygen into air sacks connected to the lungs. We see this system in modern birds.

QUETZALCOATLUS

PTERANODON

ARGENTAVIS

A FLIGHT OF MONSTERS

Pteranodon has long been thought of as the largest of the pterosaurs. The biggest species of *Pteranodon* had a wingspan of about 30 feet (9 m). In the 1970s, however, remains from an even larger pterosaur were found in Upper Cretaceous rocks in Texas. It was given the name *Quetzalcoatlus*, after the flying serpent from Aztec mythology. All sorts of estimates were made about the size of this beast. The current estimate is that it had a wingspan of about 36–39 feet (11–12 m). The biggest bird known is the condorlike *Argentavis* from Argentina, which existed around 35 million years ago. It had a wingspan of 25 feet (7.5 m). Among living birds, the royal albatross has the biggest wingspan, reaching 10 feet (3 m).

TRIASSIC	EARLY/MID JURASSIC	LATE JURASSIC	EARLY CRETACEOUS	LATE CRETACEOUS
248-206 MYA	206-159 MYA	159-144 MYA	144-97 MYA	97-65 MYA

THE FIRST BIRD

In 1859, Charles Darwin published *The Origin of Species* and created a sensation. How could animals have evolved into different types over a long period if they had all been created at one time, as it says in the Bible? The scientific community found itself in opposition to the overpowering influence of traditional biblical teaching. Then, two years later, a remarkable fossil was discovered in the quarries of Solnhofen (see pages 12–13). It was obviously a dinosaur, but it featured bird's wings and was covered with feathers. Here were the remains of a creature that appeared to represent a stage in the evolution of birds from dinosaurs. Today, few scientists dispute the notion that *Archaeopteryx* (as this creature was named) evolved from dinosaur ancestors.

THE LIVING ARCHAEOPTERYX

Had we seen *Archaeopteryx* in life, fluttering away from us, there would be no doubt in our minds that we were looking at a bird, though a rather clumsy one. However, a closer look would reveal a set of toothed jaws, as in a dinosaur, instead of the usual bird beak. The tail appeared to be paddle-shaped, unlike a modern bird's muscular stump with a bunch of feathers. This tail was a stiff, straight rod, like a dinosaur's tail, with feathers growing from each side. The final oddity would be the claws, three of them protruding from the leading edge of the wing. All in all, *Archaeopteryx* would have appeared part bird, part dinosaur.

VINDICATING DARWIN

Ten *Archaeopteryx* fossils have been found so far, all from the Solnhofen quarries, ranging in quality from a single feather to an almost complete bony skeleton with feathers. One was found in a private collection, having been misidentified as the small dinosaur *Compsognathus*. This specimen did not show the feathers, and the misidentification points out the resemblance between primitive birds and their dinosaur ancestors.

FEATHER

The first *Archaeopteryx* fossil to be found was no more than a feather. By itself, it looks like nothing unusual. It is a perfectly conventional flight feather as found on a modern bird. The main support is a vane that is off-center, showing that it is from a wing and used for flight. The filaments forming the vane of the feather had rows of hooks that enabled them to connect with one another and give stability—just as in a modern bird. A downy portion at the base provided insulation — also as in birds. About a year later, the first partial *Archaeopteryx* skeleton was found.

THE WING

The wing of *Archaeopteryx* was no halfway measure. Apart from the clawed fingers, it was identical in structure to the wing of a modern flying bird, with the elongated fingerlike primary feathers, bunched secondaries, and coverts streamlining the whole structure. The wing muscles would have been weaker than those of a modern bird, since there was no strong breastbone to anchor them. But the flying action must have been the same.

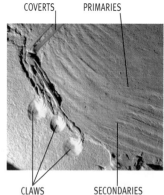

COVERTS   PRIMARIES

CLAWS   SECONDARIES

TRIASSIC 248-206 MYA	EARLY/MID JURASSIC 206-159 MYA	LATE JURASSIC 159-144 MYA	EARLY CRETACEOUS 144-97 MYA	LATE CRETACEOUS 97-65 MYA

CHINESE "GANG OF THREE"

Across the contemporary European-Asian landmass, where China's Liaoning Province now lies, a series of forest-shrouded inland lakes produced fossils that were just as spectacular as those from Solnhofen. These include three kinds of animal that, like *Archaeopteryx*, show the evolutionary connection between birds and dinosaurs. Only recently, with improved scientific exchanges between China and the West, has their significance been fully appreciated.

SINOSAUROPTERYX

One of the little dinosaurs present in Liaoning Province was *Sinosauropteryx*. It seems to have been covered with fur or feathers. The fossil preservation is so good that a kind of downy fuzz is visible around the bones. Although there is still some dissent, most scientists are convinced that this represents a covering of "protofeathers," structures partway between hair, like that of a mammal, and feathers, like those of a bird.

SINOSAUROPTERYX FOSSIL

Only the downy covering on this skeleton shows *Sinosauropteryx* to have been related to the birds. Apart from that, it is pure meat-eating dinosaur. The long legs and tail show it to have been a swift-running animal, while the short arms displayed three claws. Three skeletons of *Sinosauropteryx* have been found, and their stomach contents show that they hunted lizards and small mammals.

HALF-BIRD, HALF-DINOSAUR

Another small animal was *Protarchaeopteryx*. It was about the same size as *Sinosauropteryx*, but it had a short tail and much longer arms. It was also covered with fuzz, and although the only skeleton found was very jumbled, there seemed to be long feathers along the arms and tail. The feathers on the arms would have given a winglike structure, but it would not have been sufficient to give the animal any power of flight.

MANIRAPTORAN DINOSAURS

The group of meat-eating dinosaurs known as the maniraptorans has always been viewed as birdlike. Attempts have been made to put them on the ancestral tree of the birds, but the problem is that, being Late Cretaceous dinosaurs, they lived much later than *Archaeopteryx*, which most scientists consider the first bird. Perhaps the maniraptorans evolved from *Archaeopteryx* or *Archaeopteryx*-like birds that lost their ability to fly. If that were true, they would have been very much like the Chinese "Gang of Three."

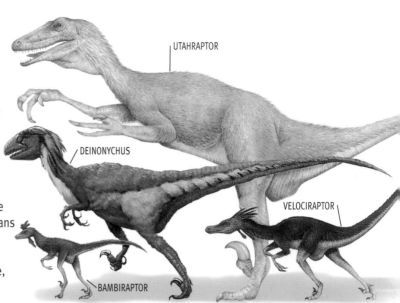

UTAHRAPTOR

DEINONYCHUS

VELOCIRAPTOR

BAMBIRAPTOR

CAUDIPTERYX'S ENVIRONMENT

Caudipteryx (see above, bottom right-hand corner), part of the Chinese "Gang of Three," lived in an environment like the one shown above. Forests of conifers and ginkgoes, with an undergrowth of ferns and cycads, provided refuge and food for many different animals in Late Jurassic and Early Cretaceous China. Lizards and small mammals scampered through the undergrowth, and little feathered theropod dinosaurs hunted between the trees. The air was colonized by birds (some resembling modern types), while on the ground raced several different half-dinosaur, half-bird creatures.

TRIASSIC 248-206 MYA	EARLY/MID JURASSIC 206-159 MYA	LATE JURASSIC 159-144 MYA	EARLY CRETACEOUS 144-97 MYA	LATE CRETACEOUS 97-65 MYA

TOWARD MODERN BIRDS

For all its fine feathers, *Archaeopteryx* was still mostly dinosaur. It had a long reptilian tail, fingers on the wings, and a jaw full of teeth. Modern birds have stumpy tails called pygostyles supporting long feathers. Their wing fingers have completely disappeared, and they also have beaks instead of jaws and teeth. These are all weight-saving adaptations, evolved to make the bird as light as possible so that it can fly more efficiently. These features seem to have appeared at different times during the time of the dinosaurs.

THE FIRST BEAK

Confuciusornis is the first beaked bird that we know of. A beak is a much more practical, lightweight alternative to the heavy teeth and jaws of a reptile. It consists of a sliver of bone, sheathed in a lightweight, horny substance that combines strength with lightness. Anything that reduces weight is an advantage to a flying animal.

A MODERN TAIL

Iberomesornis, a fossil bird from Upper Cretaceous rocks in Spain, is the earliest bird known to have a pygostyle tail. This structure consists of a muscular stump from which the tail feathers grow in a fan arrangement. The muscles of the pygostyle can spread the tail feathers out or bunch them together, helping control flight or make a display for courting purposes.

THE PERCHING FOOT

Birds that live in trees usually have feet in which the first toe is turned backward, enabling the foot to grasp a small branch so the bird can perch. An early example of a perching foot is found in *Changchengornis*, a close relative of *Confuciusornis* that is also found in the Liaoning rocks. This bird also had a hooked beak, suggesting that it was a meat eater, like a modern hawk.

TRIASSIC 248-206 MYA	EARLY/MID JURASSIC 206-159 MYA	LATE JURASSIC 159-144 MYA	EARLY CRETACEOUS 144-97 MYA	LATE CRETACEOUS 97-65 MYA

CONFUCIUSORNIS FOSSIL

Many hundreds of fossils of *Confuciusornis* have been uncovered at the Liaoning site in China. Some are so well preserved that the details of the plumage are clear. Some have long tail feathers, like those of a bird of paradise, while others have none. This suggests that, like modern birds, the males had much more flamboyant plumage than the females.

FLIGHT CONTROL

Eoalulavis, from Early Cretaceous lake deposits in Spain, is the first bird that we know to have carried an alula. An alula is a tuft of feathers on the leading edge of the wing, more or less where our thumb is. With very small movements of this structure, the passage of air over the wing can be altered considerably, and this makes flight much more controllable. Although all modern birds have this feature, fossils of *Eoalulavis* are unclear about whether the bird had other advanced features, such as a beak or a pygostyle.

ALULA

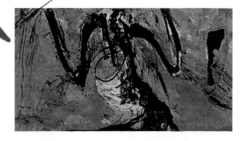

ABANDONING FLIGHT

It seems to some scientists that often no sooner has a feature evolved than certain lines of evolution abandon it. As soon as flight evolved, some birds reverted to living on the ground. There are several explanations for this. Perhaps flightless birds evolved in areas where no dangerous predators lived on the ground, and so there was no need to fly, or perhaps food was more plentiful on the ground.

KILLER DUCK

Bullockornis lived in Australia around 20 million years ago. It stood 10 feet (3 m) high and had a huge beak that was used for either cracking nuts or tearing flesh. An enlarged brain capacity suggests that the latter was more likely, since quick senses are necessary for hunting prey. *Bullockornis* was unrelated to the emus or the cassowaries or to any other type of flightless bird that exists in Australia today. Despite its dinosaur-like appearance, *Bullockornis* was actually a kind of duck.

PLANT EATERS

Not only were the shapes of the meat-eating dinosaurs reflected in some of the later birds, but bird versions of the long-necked plant eaters seem to have existed as well. *Dinorinis*, the moa, existed in New Zealand up to modern times. It thrived there because no ground-living predators lived in New Zealand—until human beings came along and wiped out the bird.

HESPERORNIS BONES

Hesperornis was a swimming bird of Late Cretaceous North America. As big as a human, it must have looked something like a penguin, but with no forelimbs at all and a long beak full of teeth. This leg bone was found in chalk deposits in western Kansas.

DEAD AS A DODO

Probably the best known of the extinct, flightless birds is *Raphus*, the dodo. The dodo evolved from pigeon stock into a ground-dwelling plant eater on the island of Mauritius. It survived there for thousands of years, as there were no ground-living predators. Everything changed, however, when humans arrived on the island, and the bird was wiped out within a few years.

THE DINOCAUN RE-EVOLVED?

A number of huge, flightless, hunting birds evolved around 65 million years ago, once the dinosaurs died out. *Phorusrhachos* of South America and *Diatryma* of North America were built along the lines of medium-sized meat-eating dinosaurs, with fast hind legs and fierce heads. *Titanis* (right) from Florida even had tiny clawed hands on the remains of its wings—almost as if a niche developed for dinosaur-shaped hunting creatures and evolution filled it with giant hunting birds.

LATE CRETACEOUS 97-65 MYA	PALEOGENE 65-23 MYA	NEOGENE 23-1.8 MYA	QUATERNARY 1.8-0.01 MYA

SINCE THE DINOSAURS

The end of the Cretaceous Period was marked by a mass extinction. The birds were a bit luckier than other creatures. They lost three-quarters of their species, but the remaining one-quarter soon re-established themselves as the masters of the skies. As the mammals spread in the absence of dinosaurs, they also took to the skies. The bats developed successfully, and other mammal groups developed gliding forms. There were even gliding reptiles and amphibians. Throughout all this, insects continued to buzz, as they have done since Carboniferous times.

THE WEBBED WAY

The birds that survived the mass extinction went on to become the true masters of the skies. Birds today mostly fly, but they can also perch, wade, swim, and even burrow. *Presbyornis* was a long-legged wading duck that lived in huge flocks in North America around 65 million years ago. Although it had webbed feet, its legs would have been too long to allow it to swim. The webs probably developed to prevent it from sinking into the mud.

MODERN GLIDERS

Today, gliding squirrels (right) float from tree to tree by means of flaps of skin (patagia) between their limbs. This is not a new development. In lake deposits in Germany, a well-preserved fossil of a gliding mammal around 23 million years old has been found. Only 4 inches (10 cm) long, *Eomys* shows evidence of patagia between the limbs. It was a kind of rodent, like a squirrel.

LATE CRETACEOUS 97-65 MYA	PALEOGENE 65-23 MYA	NEOGENE 23-1.8 MYA	QUATERNARY 1.8-0.01 MYA

AN EARLY BAT

In the Early Tertiary, not
long after the extinction of
the pterosaurs, bats appeared.
Icaronycteris would have been almost
indistinguishable from modern bats. The only
differences were the primitive teeth, the claw
on the thumb and the first finger (modern bats
only have a claw on the thumb), and the long
tail that was not connected to the hind legs
by the web of skin. In modern bats, the tail
is completely joined to the wing membrane.

THE TRUE KINGS

Insects appeared nearly 400 million years ago
and immediately evolved flying types. Few died
out in the mass extinction at the end of the
Cretaceous, and they are now far more diverse
than any other group of creatures. Wings are the
tough parts of an insect's anatomy, and it is
mostly wings that have been fossilized.
Occasionally the preservation is so good that
the patterns and markings are preserved,
although the colors have long since changed.

DID YOU KNOW?

The first scientific drawing of the skull of *Dimorphodon* (*see page 16*) was done in 1828 by Joseph Anning, brother of the famous fossil collector Mary Anning. He actually used the ink from fossilized belemnite shells found in the same beds as the *Dimorphodon* remains. Belemnites were relatives of the squid that lived during Jurassic and Cretaceous times.

Rhamphorhynchoids are usually shown with a diamond-shaped vane on the end of the tail (*see pages 14–19*). In fact several well-preserved specimens of *Rhamphorhynchus* itself do show this. However, some specimens of *Rhamphorhynchus* show a triangular vane, like the diamond but chopped off at the end. Other related rhamphorhynchoids show a long narrow paddle-shaped vane. The trouble is that in the overwhelming majority of specimens the vane, if it existed, is not preserved. Perhaps there was a vast range of vane shapes, and we usually just go for the diamond-shape because that is best known.

The first record of a pterosaur being studied dates from 1764 when Cosimo Collini investigated a fossil that had been found in a closet in the palace of Mannheim.

We really do not know how pterosaurs evolved. They seem to fly fully formed into the geological record, complete with their peculiar wings. It is hardly surprising. Something as lightweight and delicate as a flying animal is very unlikely to become fossilized after death, and so the odds against anything like this becoming a fossil are enormous. In fact, we are very lucky to have the pterosaur specimens that do exist.

There was a small relative of *Pteranodon* (*see page 24*) called *Nyctosaurus* that lived at the same time in the same area. It was very similar to its larger relative but the skull lacked the distinctive crest. Recently more complete specimens have been found and these show that there was a crest after all, but a very delicate one that was rarely preserved. This crest was branched, like a tree or a deer's antler, and was so big that it was almost the size of the wings. We do not know the purpose of this crest. It may have been used only for display, or it may have had skin stretched between the branches and been used as some kind of flight control mechanism. The investigation goes on.

The birds that co-existed with the dinosaurs in Cretaceous times were mostly not all that different from those that exist today. Genetic studies of modern birds show that the ancestors of the main groups were established back then. So, the environment of *Tyrannosaurus* and *Triceratops* was shared with the anseriformes (the ducks and geese), the galliformes (the hens) and the ratites (the big flightless birds). These survived the great extinction at the end of the Cretaceous and are still with us today.

Unlike pterosaur wing membranes or bird feathers, insect wings are quite robust. They are the most common insect parts that are found as fossils. Another reason for this is that there is no food on an insect's wing, and so an insectivorous animal will usually discard the wings as it eats the rest of it.

The best fossils of flying insects are of those trapped in amber. The most abundant of these date from Oligocene times, 35–40 million years ago — long after the age of the dinosaurs.

We have very few fossils that show the evolution of the insects and of flight. They seem to have evolved in early Silurian times, about 430 million years ago, but after that the first 85 million years of their history are only known from four fossils that have so far been found. The earliest impression of a flying insect dates from the Pennsylvanian period about 310 million years ago. It is a trace fossil from mudstones in Massachusetts, and consists merely of the impression of an insect that landed, splat!, into soft mud and left its impression behind as it took off again.

SUMMARY TIMELINE

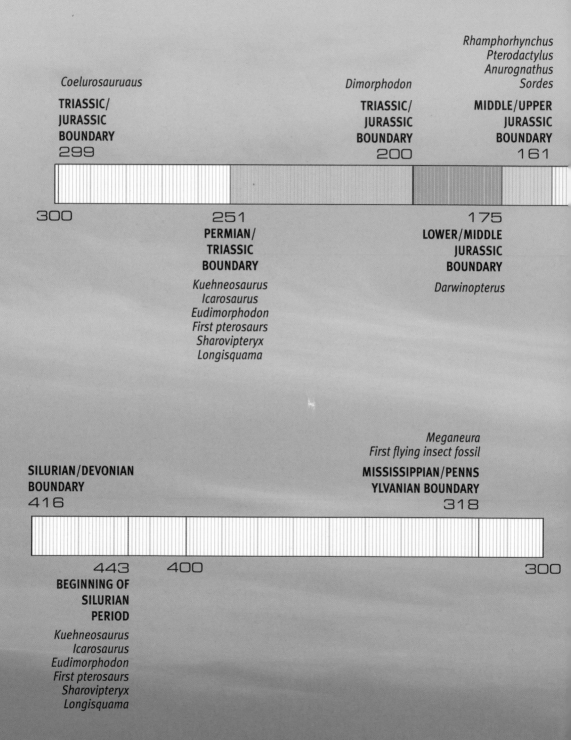

Coelurosauruaus

**TRIASSIC/
JURASSIC
BOUNDARY**
299

Dimorphodon

**TRIASSIC/
JURASSIC
BOUNDARY**
200

*Rhamphorhynchus
Pterodactylus
Anurognathus
Sordes*

**MIDDLE/UPPER
JURASSIC
BOUNDARY**
161

300

251
**PERMIAN/
TRIASSIC
BOUNDARY**

*Kuehneosaurus
Icarosaurus
Eudimorphodon
First pterosaurs
Sharovipteryx
Longisquama*

175
**LOWER/MIDDLE
JURASSIC
BOUNDARY**

Darwinopterus

*Meganeura
First flying insect fossil*

**SILURIAN/DEVONIAN
BOUNDARY**
416

**MISSISSIPPIAN/PENNS
YLVANIAN BOUNDARY**
318

443
**BEGINNING OF
SILURIAN
PERIOD**

400

300

*Kuehneosaurus
Icarosaurus
Eudimorphodon
First pterosaurs
Sharovipteryx
Longisquama*

Hesperornis
Pteranodon
Nyctosaurus
Arambourgiania
Quetzalcoatlus
Hatzegopterus
Velociraptor
Bambiraptor
Most modern bird families established
Ornithocheirus

LOWER/UPPER
CRETACEOUS
BOUNDARY
99

ICARONYCTERIS

145

100

65

0

JURASSIC/
CRETACEOUS
BOUNDARY

UPPERCRETACEOUS/
TERTIARY BOUNDARY

million
years
ago

Deinonychus
Utahraptor
Tapejara
Tupuxuara
Dsungasripterus
Microraptor
Iberomesornis
Eoalulavis
Nemicolopterus
Sinornis
Caudipteryx
Protarchaeopteryx
Sinosauropteryx
Confuciusornis
Changchengornis

Raphus
Dinornis
Titanis
Phorusrhachos
Bullockornis
Argentavis
Abundant insect fossils in amber
Diatryma
Icaronycteris
Eomys
Presbyornis

BULLOCKORNIS

DSUNGASRIPTERUS

WHERE DID THEY LIVE?

We usually think of the pterosaurs as being fish-eating animals. This is largely because we only know them from remains fossilized in sediments laid down in water. And flying animals that lived by water are very likely to have been fish eaters. We know next to nothing about pterosaurs that lived inland or in mountainous areas. Remains tend not to fossilize in such areas. There was probably a vast range of pterosaur types that lived away from the water, and these would have had all sorts of diets and lifestyles, and shapes of heads and jaws that were adapted to that. We shall never know the full range of pterosaur types.

The earliest-known pterosaurs hail from northern Italy. In late Triassic times this region was on the northern shores of a huge gulf known as the Tethys ocean. The supercontinent of Pangaea—incorporating all the landmasses of the globe—existed at that time, and the Tethys Ocean almost cut it in half, separating the northern part, called Laurasia, from the southern part, called Gondwana. Fossils found preserved in the sediments that were gathering along the northern shoreline consisted of all sorts of reptiles, including the early rhamphorhynchoids like *Eudimorphodon* and *Peteinosaurus*. They may have lived elsewhere but so far there have been no other pterosaur fossils found from this time.

The Jurassic pterosaurs of North America are not well known. The sediments of the Morrison Formation have yielded individual bones which, when compared to the more complete fossils from Solnhofen, show that both rhamphorhynchoid and pterodactyloid pterosaurs shared this landscape with the greatest dinosaurs of the time.

As we have seen, the best place for finding late Jurassic pterosaurs is in the lagoon limestones of Solnhofen in Germany (*see pages 12–13*). Again this was at the northern edge of the Tethys Ocean.

From rocks formed at the beginning of the Cretaceous period the best locality for pterosaur remains is Jehol in China. There the quiet waters of inland lakes, poisoned by the outpourings of nearby volcanoes, preserved the remains of many small animals of the time. These included tiny feathered dinosaurs, including the gliding *Microraptor*, gliding lizards, many pterosaurs, and a dizzying array of early birds. The birds showed all sorts of transitional features between those of dinosaurs and those of present day birds. Some had long lizard-like tails, some had the short modern-type tail. Some had claws on the wings, some had not. Some had jaws with teeth, some had beaks. It was almost as if evolution were trying out all sorts of things to see what worked.

Birds were around in North America in the early Cretaceous as well. Much of the mid-west was covered by an inland sea at this time, and the north-south shoreline to the west of this was a migration route for plant-eating dinosaurs. We know this because of the masses of dinosaur footprints all going in the same direction, in places such as Dinosaur Ridge, just west of Denver. Here we also find the footprints of birds, that had evidently been feeding on the shoreline, pecking for worms in the sand.

The best-known pterosaur remains from the USA are also the biggest. In late Cretaceous times a shallow sea spread across the mid-west. This produced thick beds of very white limestone, called chalk. The chalk is made up of the tiny shells of microscopic floating organisms. Embedded in it are the remains of the sea reptiles that swam in these waters, and of the flying animals that flew over them. One of these was the pterodactyloid *Pteranodon*. It was first discovered in 1870, and was the first pterosaur found outside Europe. Since then there have been about 1200 specimens found, and so we know a great deal about it. With its long toothless jaws (the name means "winged and toothless") and the long crest on the back of its head, it became the popular idea of what a pterosaur looked like. It was also, with a wingspan of up to 30 feet (9 m), the largest pterosaur known and it held its record for almost a century.

That was before the discovery of Quetzalcoatlus in late Cretaceous rocks from Texas, close to the border of Mexico. Unlike *Pteranodon*, we only know of a few bones of *Quetzalcoatlus*, but these show a flying animal much bigger than *Pteranodon*, with a wingspan of possibly 39 feet (12 m).

NEW DISCOVERIES

Having always insisted that there were no flying dinosaurs, and that all the flying reptiles of dinosaur times were actually pterosaurs, we now find that there was a dinosaur that flew! More precisely, it glided. *Microraptor* was a small meat-eating dinosaur about the size of a pigeon. Its exquisitely preserved fossils from early Cretaceous lake deposits in China show flight feathers both on the forelimbs and the hind limbs. Yes, it had four wings! It could not sustain true powered flight, however, but could glide from tree to tree like a modern flying squirrel.

Records are always being broken. The smallest pterosaur now known is not *Aunurognathus* but *Nemicolopterus*, from the early Cretaceous of China. With a wingspan of about 8 inches (20 cm), this tiny insectivorous pterodactyloid was only the size of a sparrow.

A transitional form, between the primitive rhamphorhynchoids and the advanced pterodactyloids has now been discovered, in middle Jurassic rocks of China. Crow-sized *Darwinopterus* had the tail and hindquarters of a rhamphorhynchoid and the neck and head of a pterodactyloid.

Recently-discovered *Hatzegopteryx*, about the size and shape of *Quetzalcoatlus*, from the late Cretaceous of Romania, was so big that, when standing on the ground on its four legs, its long neck raised its head to the height of a giraffe.

A beautifully-preserved fossil of *Rhamphorhynchus* has shown that it breathed like a modern bird, with air sacs in the bones drawing oxygen through lungs in a more efficient way than a mammal does.

Pterosaurs flew like birds too. We can now see from footprints that as they landed they slowed their flight until they stalled, then dropped on to their hind feet, tipped over and stabilized themselves with their hands.

Pterosaurs and birds lived and fed together in early Cretaceous times, according to a slab of mudstone found in Japan. This shows the footprints of several individuals of both, wandering in a random direction, and beak marks showing that they were all probing for food.

Pterosaur eggs have now turned up in Argentina and in China. They had leathery shells, like those of crocodiles and other modern reptiles, not hard shells like birds or dinosaurs. The structure of the shell suggests that they were buried when they were laid. The adults laid them in colonies by lakesides, as modern flamingos do. The young hatched out with well-developed wings, and it seems that if the parents looked after them, then they would have done so for only a short period before they were able to look after themselves.

The South American pterosaurs with the very large head crests, such as *Tapejara* and *Tupuxuara*, are now known to have very boat-like body shapes—

streamlined with the breast bone forming a keel and the feet like stabilizers. Perhaps they spent much of their time floating on a lake surface, with their wings held vertically acting as sails. They could drift effortlessly from feeding area to feeding area in this way, perhaps steering with their huge crests.

A fossil duck from late Cretaceous rocks in Antarctica shows that birds had diversified into their major groups while the dinosaurs were still masters of the Earth.

Studies of the bones of *Archaeopteryx* shows that it was a slow-growing animal, and probably took something like two and a half years to reach adulthood. This is different from modern birds which are fully grown in a few weeks. The fast growth of modern birds probably did not evolve until early Cretaceous times, amongst the vast array of primitive birds found in China.

Birds take off by leaping from the ground with their hind legs. Pterosaurs had weak hind legs, and so to get into the air they probably leapt upward with all fours.

MOVIES, WEBSITES, & FURTHER READING

fact and how much has been made up by
the reporter. That's fun, too!

www.pterosaur.co.uk

This, the PTEROSAUR DATABASE is the
best website bar none for up-to-date
facts on pterosaurs. It can be quite
technical but it is full of useful
information.

www.pterosaur.net

This is another very good source of
information, presented a little less
formally than the PTEROSAUR DATABASE.

Google Earth

Key in SOLNHOFEN. This will take you
down to the village in Bavaria, in
southern Germany. To the west and to the
south you will see huge white patches in
the forest. These are the limestone
quarries that have produced fine-grained
thinly bedded limestone for the printing
and building industries since Roman
times. The very large patch due west of
the village, by the hamlet of
Langenaltheimer Haardt, is the main
quarry—the one from which the
Archaeopteryx specimens have been
recovered, and also many specimens of
Pterodactylus and *Rhamphorhynchus*
(see pages 10–11).

Key in MESSEL. It will take you to
another village in southern Germany. To
the south of the village, immediately
beyond the railroad track, there is a
huge, almost circular crater. It might be
rather difficult to detect because it is
covered in vegetation, but there is some
reddish disturbed ground and building
works between it and the road on the
west side. The large number of
photographs that have been uploaded
shows the importance of the place. This
is the Messel oil-shale quarry—the site

MOVIES

If dinosaurs are badly represented in
movies, then pterosaurs have an even
worse time!

Nearly all show a pterosaur to be
powerful enough and maneuverable
enough to pick up a human being in its
claws and fly off with him or her. Such
events are portrayed in *KING KONG I*
(1933), *ONE MILLION YEARS B.C.* (1966),
THE VALLEY OF GWANGI (1969), *WHEN
DINOSAURS RULED THE EARTH* (1970),
and *JURASSIC PARK III* (2001). No
pterosaur, no matter how big and
powerful, could have done this. Nor could
it have picked up a human in its jaws, as
in *THE LAND THAT TIME FORGOT* (1975).

Special effects artists who should know
better even give pterosaurs bats' wings,
as in *ONE MILLION YEARS B.C.* and *THE
VALLEY OF GWANGI.* (Both used the same
model, so it is really a single fault).

WEBSITES

Wikipedia tends to be distrusted by many
people because it is too easy to put
spurious information on it. However, the
dinosaur material published there is
generally quite reliable and up to date.

www.dinosaursociety.com

All sorts of information on dinosaurs,
including a valuable frequently updated
page giving links to all the dinosaur-
related news stories.

www.sciencedaily.com/news/
fossils_ruins/dinosaurs/

A catalog of the dinosaur stories run by
this news site.

Warning! *The articles presented by these
sites are usually written by journalists,
not by dinosaur specialists. As a result
they tend to be over-sensational or
sometimes plain wrong. If you find an
interesting dinosaur news story, it is
oa good idea to chase it up through
different sources, to see how the story
differs. Usually, you can tell how much is*

of the tertiary crater lake, in which all kinds of small mammals and birds have been fossilized. This is where the specimens of the bat *Icaronycteris* and the gliding mouse *Eomys* were discovered.

Key in LOGAN COUNTY KANSAS. This is the area in which the first *Pteranodon* specimens were found, back in 1870 (*see page 24*). Flowing west to east across the county is the Smoky Hill River, and you can see the steep sides of the river with the rock strata exposed. Now key in CHALK BUTES, MANVILLE and it will move you to an area in Wyoming in which the same chalk rocks outcrop, and you will see them nicely as buttes and cliffs. This whole area— Kansas, Wyoming, Nebraska —was covered in a shallow ocean in late Cretaceous times, and *Pteranodon* fossils are found all over.

Key in BIG BEND NATIONAL PARK. This rocky desert area on the Texas side of the Mexico border is the site of the discovery of late Cretaceous *Quetzalcoatlus*— one of the biggest of the pterosaurs.

FURTHER READING

THE ILLUSTRATED ENCYCLOPEDIA OF PTEROSAURS

Wellnhofer, P., 1991 Salamander

Probably the best popular level book on the subject ever, with fabulous artwork by John Sibbick. May be a little dated but still perfectly valid.

THE DINOSAURIA
Edited by David B. Weishampel, Peter Dodson, and Halszka Osmólska, 2nd edition 2004

This is the bible for paleontologists. However, it is extremely technical and hardly to be recommended for the casual reader. And, since the science is constantly changing, the 2nd edition may well be out of date already.

PREHISTORIC TIMES
A quarterly magazine, running since 1993, features articles on dinosaur research and dinosaur lore. See their website *www.prehistorictimes.com*

GLOSSARY

Alula A small bunch of feathers on the leading edge of a bird's wing that helps to control the flight.

Amber Fossilized resin, often used as jewellery.

Aztec One of the ancient cultures of Mexico, before the arrival of Europeans.

Beak A lightweight horny structure forming the mouth of some animals such as birds.

Carboniferous The period of geological time from 354 to 290 million years ago. The time of the coal forests.

Carnivore An animal that eats meat.

Crest A structure on the head of an animal, used for display. A crest may be made of bone, horn, or feathers.

Cretaceous The period of geological time from 144 to 65 million years ago. The last of the three dinosaur periods.

Cycad A plant with the appearance of a palm but more closely related to the conifers.

Digestive system The collection of organs in the body that processes food —the stomach, and intestines.

Dinosaur One of a group of reptiles that existed from the Triassic to the Cretaceous periods of Earth history.

Display When one animal shows off to another, either to attract mates or to scare away enemies.

DNA Deoxyribonucleic acid. The chemical which determines the genetic development of an animal.

Down A fuzzy feathery covering used as insulation.

Environment The total of all the surroundings in which an animal or a plant lives—the climate, the vegetation, the terrain, and so on.

Evolve To change from one type of animal to another over generations, in response to changing condition.

Excavate To dig up.

Fossilize To turn to stone. An organism becomes fossilized when its organic material changes to mineral material after being buried for a long time in rock.

Glide To fly by catching the air on spread wings and sliding along it.

Jurassic The period of geological time between 206 and 144 million years ago. The heyday of the dinosaurs.

Lagerstatte (Plural lagerstaten) A fossil locality that is so well preserved that everything about the fossils and their living conditions can be determined from it.

Magma Molten rock from beneath the earth's surface.

Mammal A warm-blooded animal, usually covered in fur, that gives birth to live offspring and suckles its young.

Maniraptoran One of a group of small or medium-sized hunting theropods with strong grasping hands.

Omnivorous Able to eat both plants and animals.

Paleontologist A scientist who studies paleontology.

Paleontology (Spelled "palaeontology" in Europe) The study of the life of the past.

Permian The period of geological time from 290 to 248 million years ago. Reptiles were dominant on the land but the dinosaurs had not yet evolved.

Plumage The covering of feathers on a bird.

Prehistoric From before human history.

Pterosaur One of a group of flying reptiles related to the dinosaurs.

Pterodactyloid One of the two major groups of pterosaur, with short tails, long wrist bones, and long necks.

Reptile A cold-blooded animal that reproduces by laying eggs, and is usually covered by a scaly skin. Lizards and snakes are typical modern reptiles.

Resin A sticky substance that oozes from the bark of trees.

Rhamphorhynchoid One of the two major groups of pterosaur, with long tails, short wrist bones, and short necks.

Skull The assemblage of bones in the head.

Solar panel A device that catches the heat of the sun.

Theory A selection of ideas that can be tested scientifically.

Theropod The group of dinosaurs to which all meat-eaters belong.

Triassic The period of geological time between 248 and 206 million years ago, that saw the beginning of the age of dinosaurs.

Vertebrae The bones of the neck, back, and tail.

INDEX

Africa 13, 20, 22
amphibians 9, 34, 36
Anning, Mary 16
Anurognathus 24
Arambourgiania 24
Archaeopteryx 26, 27, 28, 29, 31, 36
Argentavis 25
Asia 8, 9, 29
Australia 32

Bambiraptor 29
bats 5, 10, 11, 16, 18, 34, 35
beaks 16, 21, 22, 26, 30, 31, 32, 33, 41
birds 4, 5, 6, 7, 9, 11, 13, 15, 16, 18, 20, 22, 25, 26–34, 36, 41, 42
Bullockornis 32

Carboniferous Period 4, 6, 34
Caudipteryx 29
Changchengornis 30
China 22, 28–29, 31, 41, 42, 43
Coelurosauravus 7, 9
Compsognathus 26
Confuciusornis 30, 31
crests 22–23, 36, 41, 42, 43
Cretaceous Period 5, 7, 14, 18, 6, 15, 22, 24, 25, 29, 31, 33, 34, 35, 36, 41, 42, 43
Cuvier, Georges 10

Darwin, Charles 21, 26
De la Beche, Sir Henry 10
Deinonychus 29
Diatryma 33
Dimorphodon 16
Dinornis 32
Dsungaripterus 22

Eoalulavis 31
Eomys 34
Eudimorphodon 14, 15
Europe 13, 28
  England 9, 10, 11, 16, 20
  Germany 10, 12, 13, 18, 34, 40
    Solnhofen 10, 12–13, 18, 21, 26, 28, 40
  Romania 12, 42
  Spain 12, 30, 31
evolution 9, 15, 20, 21, 26, 28, 32, 33, 34, 36, 37, 41

fish 7, 11, 15, 17, 20, 22, 23, 36
fossils 6, 9, 10, 11, 12, 13, 14, 18, 19, 20, 26, 28, 30, 31, 34, 35, 36, 37, 40, 42

Hawkins, Thomas 11
Hesperornis 33

Iberomesornis 30
Icaronycteris 35
Icarosaurus 8, 9
ichthyosaurs 11
insects 4, 6, 21, 22, 24, 34, 35, 37

Jurassic Period 10, 13, 14, 16, 17, 19, 20, 22, 24, 29, 36, 40, 42

Kuehneosaurus 9

Longisquama 9

mammals 5, 6, 11, 28, 29, 34, 35, 36
maniraptorans 29
marsupials 11
Martin, John 11
Mauritius 33
Meganeura 6

New Zealand 32
Newman, Edward 11
North America 33, 34, 40, 41

Permian Period 7, 8
Phorusrhachos 33
plesiosaurs 11
Presbyornis 34
Protarchaeopteryx 28
Pteranodon 23, 24, 25, 36, 41

pterodactyloids 14, 17, 20, 22, 40, 42
pterodactyls 11, 20
Pterodactylus 20, 21
pterosaurs 6–8, 10–19, 21–25, 35, 36, 40, 42, 43

Quetzalcoatlus 25, 41, 42

Raphus 33
reptiles 4, 6–11, 30, 34, 40, 41, 42
  lizards 5, 6, 7, 8, 9, 13, 16, 28, 29, 41
rhamphorhynchoids 14, 16, 17, 19, 20, 24, 36, 40, 42
Rhamphorhynchus 18, 20, 36, 42

Sharovipteryx 8, 9
Sinornis 7
Sinosauropteryx 28
Sordes 19
South America 16, 25, 33, 42

Tapejara 23, 42
Tertiary Period 35
Tethys Ocean 12, 13, 40
theropods 29
Titanis 33
Titanopteryx 24
Triassic Period 5, 7, 8, 9, 14
Tropeognathus 23
Tupuxuara 23, 42

United States 9, 24, 25, 32
Utahraptor 29

Velociraptor 29

Wagler, Johann 11

ACKNOWLEDGMENTS

The original publisher would like to thank Advocate and Elizabeth Wiggans for their assistance.

Picture Credits: t=top, b=bottom, c=center, l=left, r=right
Lisa Alderson: 8b, 17b, 18–19c, 24l, 28b, 29t, 33bl. John Alston: 12l, 12–13b, 13tr, 14–15c, 15cr, 15b, 19t.
BBC Natural History Unit: 18cl. Corbis: 12t, 18b, 20c. Dr. Peter Griffiths: 26t, 26b, 27r. Simon Mendez:
6–7b, 8–9c, 16–17, 17t, 20–21c, 22t, 29t, 30t, 31t, 31b, 32–33, 34l. National Museum of Wales: 11, 22b.
Natural History Museum: 7t, 10t, 14b, 16t, 20t, 25r, 33t. Paleontologisk Museum, Oslo: 8cl, 9cr, 30cr.
Luis Rey: 9b, 14tl, 21, 22–23c, 24–25, 26–27, 28t, 29bl, 32l, 34–35.

Every effort has been made to trace the copyright holders
and we apologize in advance for any unintentional errors or omissions.

NOTE TO READERS
The website addresses are correct at the time of publishing. However, due to the ever-changing nature
of the Internet, websites and content may change. Some websites can contain links that are unsuitable
for children. The publisher is not responsible for changes in content or website addresses. We advise
that Internet searches should be supervised by an adult.